break the cycle

by **Alice Ashcroft**

The nurse that told me to "focus on the positives" of my autism, asked me if I thought I was a good person.

"No", I answered, "but I don't think anyone is. I think we like to trick ourselves into thinking we are by doing things that make us feel better about our lives. I think if we were good people, there wouldn't be genocide, starvation, racism, gender pay gaps, and the environment wouldn't be a mess. So this is less about if I'm a good person, and whether or not people are capable of being good."

Later, when I made a comment that I'd ticked a box, she told me it wasn't about "ticking boxes" but "meeting the criteria".

I laughed in her face.

I didn't feel guilty about that. Proving my point.

Had a breakdown, planned to disappear,
and still didn't cry.
Signed off work and let people down.
Volunteered at a school.
Laughed at a nurse when she told me it wasn't about
"ticking boxes" but "meeting the criteria".
Cleaned the kitchen.
Chased the doctors.
Did some washing.
Chased the doctors.
Did some laundry.
Ordered tile samples.
Read a book.
Read another.
Thought about chasing the doctors.
Still can't seem to cry.

The Doctor might see you now.

I feel like I've spent the last ten years running.
Not literally, my joints don't work.
But I feel like I've been focusing on the next thing,
all the time, without taking a moment to figure out what
that should be.
TikTok told me I "consider success only through
academic validation".
And even now, I'm the doctor in question,
I'm still not listening.

A week or so before the burnout, I went out for some drinks.
My hair was great and I wore a new jumpsuit.
Expectations rarely meet reality.

A fantastic book.
"really good, actually"
It randomly cuts to "fantasies", so here's mine.

You wake up, and it's warm outside, but you slept well, the heat didn't disturb you. Your toddler has decided to have a lie in (unthinkable in reality, but go with me), so you cuddle up to your partner and take a minute to remember the incredible night before. You wander downstairs, and make a chai latte, and without trying it's perfect. When your toddler eats his breakfast, he doesn't get weetabix stuck to everything, because if he did it would dry like concrete and you'd spend three hours cleaning it up every week instead of just wiping it off before it dries.

You saunter over to the local bakery, and buy five croissants for a family of three, because nobody judges you and you've got a really healthy relationship with food and your body. It's telling you what it needs. You sit by the side of the lake, I guess you live by a lake, and you eat your breakfast. Your dog chases birds but in a cute fun way not in a "ooh sorry, she's not normally like that" kind of way. Your child plays safely, somehow this perfectly natural landscape is completely toddler-proof. You can work later, if you want. You love your work but there's no deadlines. You can sit in the sun, and even though you're ginger you won't burn, for as long as you like.

When you get home, the house is tidy and clean, as if by magic.

I cry a lot.
More than most, I think.
But when I become emotionally numb, the only thing that seemed to break me is someone "needing space". Maybe that's the space I needed to break down and cry.

Feeling trapped might not be unusual for somebody who is neuro-divergent.
Some might call it "decision paralysis".
I might call it "not realising how you feel about a situation until it's all too much, and it's making you physically ill".

Sometimes, it's everything all together that makes you feel trapped.
Sometimes, it's getting water on your sock.

You're told, by people who try their best to understand, that it's a "super power".
That it's "a way of making yourself feel better about your faults".
"Why do you need to label it?"
"Everyone's a little bit autistic."
"You have ADHD now, too?"
"You're making yourself stand out."

"Help" you want to scream, whilst listing the research and laws in your head.

"We're all neuro-diverse" I see on a book cover and it makes my skin itch.
Until I realise the difference between "diverse" and "divergent".

But do these labels trap me?
Or is it the traits themselves?
Because even without the labels, I felt trapped.
But now, at least, I know why.

                                        I think I want to.
                            But sometimes I'm not too sure.
                                Run away, fly away, gone.

I started writing, I started crying.
I started singing, but my voice was too dry.
I started recording,
but I didn't want to talk if there was nobody to listen.
I have a habit of starting things.

I'm not the first to have experienced this,
it's been happening for centuries.
"Witches, Sluts, Feminists" the effect that book had on me.
So why do I see it all from my point of view?
Am I the centre of the universe? That simply is not true.

Because I'm useless, and I'm stupid,
and my skin feels too tight.
And I'm writing pretentious bullshit
to make myself feel alright.

        Who will want to read this? People that I know?
            I hope not, that's embarrassing,
              but they're invested in the show.

           "You do so much" they say, I sing,
              but too much is not enough.

                And yet it's too much for me.

How do you take a break?
Buy yourself headphones that block out the noise.
Oh, that's your thoughts.
Watch TV that normally makes you cry.
It doesn't.
Realise who reaches out.
Realise that's not fair.
Read fiction, but it's too happy.
Read fiction, but it's too depressing.
Read non-fiction, that'll do.
Post about it online?
No, because then they'll think you're faking.
"She's well enough to read, but not well enough to work?" they might say.
Can that be true?
Okay, you'll try to work.
Nope, bad idea.
You got nothing done and forgot to eat.
Maybe you'll try and go for a walk.
But you probably won't.

Am I flakey?
Is it just my disabilities?

Am I sad?
Is it just stress?

"Everyone has ups and downs."
But are the "ups" normally mountains?
The "downs" governed by Hades?

Maybe I'm just flakey.

What are you supposed to do when you're signed off work? Are you supposed to write down your feelings in some overly dramatic way? Do laundry? Tidy the house? Finally do that painting you've not had time for?

Are you supposed to "do the work"? How do you know how to do that? Practically, what does that actually look like?

When I was ill, as a child, and off school, I had to stay in bed. Because "if you're well enough to watch TV, you're well enough to be in school". So now, I'm off work, am I allowed to watch TV? Am I allowed to meet with friends? And who is the one allowing this? Me? I suppose, I am a parent now, does that mean it's me?

But that also then means that I can't take time off. Not really. I can't lie in bed all day. I can't wallow, I just have to carry on. But not with everything, because only paid work is seen as work. And paid work is rarely the invisible labour that parents do.

Ah, there we are again.

Feminism.

Whilst scrolling I saw a trend, so thought I'd join in.

How much I made in one week as a micro-influencer:
£0.00

Smashed it.

Ten year olds are asked to write instructions at school,
as part of their English lessons.
"How to make toast."
"How to make a cup of tea."
"How to look up a word in a dictionary."

Where can I see these instructions?
I think I need help.

I often listen to music, to help myself feel.
But I've been hitting 'play' less and less.

Maybe because I already feel too much?
Maybe because I've stopped feeling at all.

"It's just a rabbit."

He was my reason for getting out of bed.
He was the way I started to grow my family.
He was just a rabbit. And so much more.

Being back at work, feels odd.
I thought I'd feel better.
I thought I'd be ready.
But maybe I never will be.

I've felt quite trapped,
but I haven't known why.

I have this compulsion,
this consistent little lie.

"I'm fine" I say,
and I try to grin.

"It's not too much."
But I have to. To win.

And it's harder to process,
when it's just in your head.

But getting things down on paper,
and not sang, but just read,

helps me feel free,
feel heard and understood.

Because if I can explain this
then maybe I should.

For years I've wanted to write a song about shadows. I think there is something quite poetic about a darker version of yourself following you around.

Putting your headphones on and finding that perfect song that encapsulates how you're feeling is amazing. How can this song writer perfectly sum up this incredibly complicated experience in one sentence? And yet with so much detail?

There's musicians like Bo Burnham who make jokes that it's because the songs are so generic. And don't get me wrong, it makes me laugh.

But if the human experience can be boiled down to being seen in just two lines of a song, then maybe we should all have more empathy. Because we clearly all feel the same.

I started thinking about this when I played my second album to myself in the car last week. I wanted something I knew I'd be able to sing. I wrote it having coped with another of my breakdowns, after finding some peace. And every single song perfectly encapsulated how I'd been feeling, or how I wanted to feel.

It made me feel hopeful, because if I've done it before, I can do it again.

I just want to break the cycle.

Book club questions.

Why did only one poem have a title?
Why are random poems in the second person?
Is this all a way of monetising a breakdown? I hope not.

Printed in Great Britain
by Amazon